Canterbury Tales

Keith Hurst

Series Editor: Andy Kempe

T

First published in 2001 by:
Nelson Thornes Ltd
Delta Place
27 Bath Road
CHELTENHAM
GL53 7TH
United Kingdom

01 02 03 04 05 / 10 9 8 7 6 5 4 3 2 1

A catalogue record for this book is available from the British
Library.

ISBN 0-7487-5694-9

Edited and typeset by Peter Nickol

Cover design by Zhenya Matysiak

Printed and bound in Great Britain by T. J. International Ltd,
Padstow, Cornwall

C O N T E N T S

ACKNOWLEDGEMENTS

Keith Hurst would like to acknowledge all those at Frogmore Community College who were involved in the original production of *Canterbury Tales* in March 1999.

Co-producer: Sue Darke.

Performers: Susan Tottman, Richard Baxter, Gareth Shaw, Alexis Humphrey, Elizabeth Webb, Katherine Walton, Aimee Kuehnel, Michael Harper, Andrew Platt, Andrew Dexter, Natalie Payne, Vicky Carr, Emma King, Holly Green, Richard Brock, Matthew Craighill, Grace Durdle, Claire White, Stephanie Basher and Claire Walker.

In production, music and design: David Webster, Bob Stone, Laura Ellis, Penny Craighill, Nigel Stevens, Wendy Griffiths, Sue Russell, Malcolm Floyd, James Walker, Katherine Walker and many others.

SuperScripts

SuperScripts is a series of plays for use in the English classroom and the Drama studio. The plays have been written by playwrights who delight in live performance and the challenges it offers to actors, designers, directors and audiences.

Most of the plays in the series were written for professional companies, but all are included because they tell stories and use techniques which will interest, excite and offer new insights to young people who are just coming to understand how drama works as an art form.

The range of plays in the series addresses the requirement to give students at Key Stages 3 and 4 an opportunity to study a variety of dramatic genres. The fact that they were all written for performance (and have indeed all been performed) means that they will also offer students the chance to understand how and why playscripts are different from novels. The Activities presented after the script are designed to draw attention to this, and to extend students' abilities in reading, writing and of course performing drama.

Many of the tasks invite students to engage directly with the text or formulate their own creative responses. Others focus on discussing, writing and designing. Both English and Drama specialists will find the series a valuable resource on which to draw in order to promote dramatic literacy – and simply performing the plays wouldn't be a bad thing either!

CANTERBURY TALES

The 24 stories which make up the *Canterbury Tales* were written over 600 years ago. Although this work was unfinished when Geoffrey Chaucer died in 1400, he had achieved enough fame as a writer to be the first person buried in the special part of Westminster Abbey which has since become known as Poets' Corner.

For Keith Hurst the idea of a story-telling competition held between such wildly different characters still seems a great one. In their original form the tales are full of energy, humour and humanity. But selecting which stories to adapt for a modern theatre audience meant considering the visual and dramatic potential of each. Perhaps it was inevitable that the funniest and rudest ones immediately seemed to suggest themselves! Chaucer had great skill, though, in balancing the ribald with the moralistic. Keith Hurst's selection recognises and uses this to create a lively entertainment which indulges people's foibles while pointing out the pitfalls of indulgence. He writes:

I adapted two stories of greedy people getting their just desserts (the Pardoner's and the Friar's), two of lust and deception (the Miller's and the Reeve's) and two which deal with the way men treat women and vice versa (the Wife of Bath's and The Nun's Priest's).

The play was originally written for a company of around twenty actors, each taking equal responsibility for bringing the tales to life. However, there are clearly opportunities for many more performers to be involved. The play offers new and stimulating challenges for the cast, and can provoke quite a response in the audience. A lot of fun can be had by having males play some of the female parts and vice versa. This helps overcome the perennial problem with school plays, where good female parts are at a premium. Cross-casting in this way can also be used to emphasise the serious point Chaucer himself seems to make about the treatment of women. There are extensive possibilities in the script for generating visual gags and 'business' while celebrating the richness and diversity of the English language. Keith Hurst again:

Chaucer wrote in rhyming couplets, but I did not attempt to copy him, except in some set-piece speeches and where the pace of speech was best suited to the pace of the action. I left a small number of speeches in the original Middle English, to give a flavour of the real thing and when the action got a bit naughty! When preparing for a production, the actors may like to consider experimenting with regional accents, especially when reciting the verse.

While a common criticism of television scheduling is that there are too many repeats, the fact that these tales can be repeated after more than 600 years must say something about them. In this adaptation, Keith Hurst has harnessed that enduring vitality and cleverly created a dramatic framework that reflects Chaucer's original while making for a wholly original and exciting play.

CANTERBURY TALES

C A S T   L I S T

Introduction

Scholar, Chaucer, Host, Fiends.

Pardoner's Tale

Pardoner, three Rioters, Potwoman, Old Man, Apothecary, Death.

Friar's Tale

Friar, Old Woman, Wench, Archdeacon, Yeoman, Summoner, Carter.

Miller's Tale

Miller, Nicholas, Alison , Absolon, Gervaise, Carpenter.

Reeve's Tale

Reeve, Miller Simkin, Wife, Daughter, Alan, John.

Wife of Bath's Tale

Wife of Bath, King, Queen, Knight, Husband, Girl, Old Woman.

Nun's Priest's Tale

Nun's Priest, Chantecleer, Pertelote, Fox, Woman, Daughters – and any number of Fiends, Lords, Ladies, Villagers and sundry animals!

ACT ONE

INTRODUCTION

*Enter **Scholar**, in modern dress, reading from a book.*

SCHOLAR   When the sweet showers of April replace
The drought of March and pierce it to the root
And every vein is bathed in that moisture…

*Enter **Chaucer**, continuing **Scholar's** speech.*

CHAUCER   …Whose quickening force will engender the flower;
Then people long to go on pilgrimages.

*(To **Scholar**.)* It sounds much better in the original,
you know.

And palmers for to seken straunge strondes
To ferne halwes, couthe in sondry londes;
And specially, from every shires ende
Of Engelond, to Caunterbury they wende
The holy blisful martir for to seke,
That hem hath holpen, whan that they were seke.

*He holds out his hand to **Scholar** – they shake as he
introduces himself.*

Geoffrey Chaucer, 1345 to 1400.

SCHOLAR   Pleased to meet you. So you had this idea of
holding a story-telling competition amongst
pilgrims on the way to Canterbury.

CHAUCER   Not me. Strictly speaking it was one of my
characters – Harry Bailly, host of the Tabard Inn at
Southwark.

*Enter **Host**, who addresses the audience.*

HOST   So you're on the way to Canterbury – and God
speed. But it is no fun travelling along the road as
dumb as stones. After all, you must treat it as a
holiday. Listen: we'll entertain each other by telling

stories, on the way there and on the way back. Just for a bit of fun, I'll come with you and judge the best. And whoever wins will be bought a meal in my very own inn by all the rest of you.

CHAUCER   *(To Scholar.)* He'll be the winner, of course – the money spent by thirty pilgrims will keep him in profit for months.

SCHOLAR   Is that why people went on pilgrimage – for a holiday?

CHAUCER   Holy day! But, yes – pilgrims were the first ever tourists. They went for new experiences, to see new people and new places.

SCHOLAR   To be forgiven their sins?

CHAUCER   As a punishment set by their priests.

SCHOLAR   To escape their dull lives.

CHAUCER   To touch the bones of a saint and be blessed.

SCHOLAR   To renew their faith.

CHAUCER   And mainly because they were terrified of going to hell.

Lights up on Hell's mouth, which sparkles and crackles. Explosions.

FIEND 1   Hell is a prison of fire that gives no light. Those in hell are piled on each other and suffer the burning flames and horrible plagues.

FIEND 2   The horror of the prison is increased by its awful stench. It smells of…

FIEND 3   …all the filth of the world in one vast reeking sewer, …

FIEND 2   …of foul air and nauseous, rotting corpses.

FIEND 1   The fire of hell was created by God to torture and punish the unrepentant sinner – it burns within and rages inside the very vitals of the soul…

FIEND 2   and all that the damned hear are the excruciating screams and curses of...

FIEND 3   ...their fellow damned. Screams which go on...

FIEND 2   and on...

FIEND 3   and on...

FIEND 2   for all eternity.

CHAUCER   As you will gather – not a wholly attractive prospect.

THE PARDONER'S TALE

SCHOLAR   *(Recovering herself.)* Weren't there such things as pardoners – who would pardon the sins of people in exchange for money?

CHAUCER   Ah, yes. We had one with us on the journey to Canterbury: *(Declaims to audience.)*
'He hadde a croys of latoun ful of stones,
And in a glas he hadde pigges bones.
But with thise relikes, whan that he fond
A poure person dwellynge up on lond,
Upon a day he gat him more moneye
Than that the person gat in monthese tweye;
And thus with feyned flaterye and japes
He made the person and the peple his apes.'

SCHOLAR   Ah-hem! *(Not understanding – bringing Chaucer back to earth.)*

CHAUCER   *(Sighs.)* He had a cheap tin cross and some pig's bones that he pretended were holy relics. He charged people for the privilege of touching them because they were said to bring blessing and good luck. Even the poorest paid up because they wanted to be saved. So he ended up making more money in a day than any good parson could hope for in two months.

Pardoner enters.

Here he is: hair like rats' tails, voice like a goat.

PARDONER *(In response – like a goat.)* Baaaa!

CHAUCER He reminds me of a castrated donkey.

Chaucer and Scholar retire to chairs/bench on side of stage.

PARDONER Gentlemen, ladies. *(Takes centre stage. Boastful.)* I swear I can shame anyone into giving me money.

He speaks directly to the audience and holds out a cloth bag.

If any of you have cheated on your wives or husbands, you are not worthy to come to me and pay for a pardon, so stay away.

Various members of the cast run on from the audience, kneel and put money in his bag.

See. *(Looks at audience.)* What about the rest of you?

Pauses for response – and, when none comes, gives a cynical laugh.

Enter Rioters, who laugh, drink and play games in the background.

But, my friends, I truly believe that Love Of Money is the root of all evil – and I have a tale to prove it.

The Rioters are lit more clearly, accepting drinks from a Potwoman.

All the youth of today want is to have fun, and this lot were no better. They drank, gambled, sang, swore and got up to all kinds of hanky panky. They were usually so out of their heads that they didn't know what they were doing. One day, they were in the tavern as usual, when…

A funeral bell tolls. Lights up on Hell's mouth. Two Fiends slowly pull a small cart, on which rests a *corpse, towards Hell's mouth. They are led by a figure of **Death**, with a black cloak, skull face and scythe. The **Fiends** lift the corpse and take it through Hell's mouth. The cart is taken back. **Death** exits through Hell's mouth. All this needs to be done by the end of the **Potwoman's** speech.*

RIOTER 1 What's that? Another corpse? *(To **Potwoman**.)* Run out and see who that is.

POTWOMAN No need. I know already. It was a friend of yours. He was sitting, drunk, last night and a thief came upon him quietly and cut him to the heart. Death is this thief's name and he's taken thousands in the latest plague. In the next village he's killed every single man, woman and child this year. You have to tread carefully and watch out for him.

RIOTER 1 Come on, he can't be that bad. I'm not going to hide away from Death. I'd rather go out and find him and kill him. Come on, you two: let's swear.

All stand.

RIOTER 2 *(Launches into an unintelligible, spluttering string of curses.)*

RIOTER 1 Not like that! Here! *(Hoists his partners' hands so that they hold fists.)* We swear…

RIOTERS 2 & 3 We swear…

RIOTER 1 …to kill Death.

RIOTERS 2 & 3 …to kill Death.

RIOTER 1 Death to Death.

RIOTERS 2 & 3 Death to Death.

*The **Fiends** enter and arrange themselves around the stage. They are carrying long branches and become the wood through which the **Rioters** walk, tripping, staggering and occasionally falling. The **Pardoner** speaks as they do this.*

PARDONER They set off towards the next village, and had gone only half a mile when they met a very old man at a narrow farm gate.

*Two **Fiends** hold two branches as the posts of the gate. The three men go through a comic routine of trying to push through all together, falling back and over.*

*The **Old Man** appears, carrying a walking stick. He is dressed in the same gown as the figure of Death seen earlier, and strolls through from the other side of the gate, quite casually.*

OLD MAN Excuse me.

RIOTER 1 *(Staggering up.)* No we won't excuse you, you old fool. *(Kicks stick from under him.)* We were here first. Get out of the way! Why should someone as old as you be walking around anyway!

*All the **Rioters** are now standing. The **Fiends** return to the Hell's mouth scaffold.*

OLD MAN I have walked to the world's end to find anyone, in any city or village, who will exchange his youth for my old age.
But of course no one will and I must remain an old man still.
Not even Death will take my life
So like a restless prisoner I pace the earth,
Knocking on it with my staff, *(Knocks.)*
Shouting loud 'Let me in! Let me in!
See how I wither, flesh, blood and skin!
When will my poor bones be at rest?'

*He pauses, then speaks to the **Rioters**.*

But sirs, you should be courteous to an old man, and treat me as you would like to be treated if you reach such old age.

RIOTER 1 Wait a minute. You just spoke of that scoundrel

Death that we have sworn to kill. Where is he? Tell us. And if you refuse, we'll treat you as his friend and kill you too.

OLD MAN   If you are so keen to meet Death, so be it. Follow this winding road *(Points.)* until you come to a stream. Beside the stream is an oak tree, old and broad, and beneath it lies what you seek. *(Exit.)*

*The three **Rioters** stagger round once more. They stop at Hell's mouth. Gold coins, thrown down by **Fiends**, rain from above. The **Rioters** kneel and show delight.*

RIOTER 2   That old fool didn't know what he was talking about. Here's the tree, but there is no Death, only gold.

RIOTER 3   We're rich.

RIOTER 1   *(Calming them down and looking thoughtful.)* Brothers, listen. Yes, we're rich. But we can't carry all this back in one go. People will think we've stolen it. We'd be fools. So I suggest this. We'll draw lots. The winner will go back to the village and buy us some bread and wine so that we can celebrate our find. The other two will stay here and guard it.

*A **Fiend** brings forward three straws and holds them out. Each of the **Rioters** takes a straw. **Rioter** 3 draws the shortest.*

PARDONER   So the youngest one lost and skipped off back to the village for bread and wine. *(**Rioter** 3 skips round and exits.)* Meanwhile…

RIOTER 1   *(To **Rioter** 2.)* Well, well, well. What a stroke of good luck, eh! This has made me so happy that I've almost sobered up.

RIOTER 2   Not to worry. The wine will soon be here.

RIOTER 1   You don't think that's the only reason I sent the poor fool away, do you? Listen. It doesn't take a bishop to work out that all this gold divided by two means more for us than if it's divided by three.

Rioter 2 *is baffled.*

RIOTER 1   *(Exasperated.)* If we get rid of him, then there's more for us.

Light slowly dawns on *Rioter 2.*

RIOTER 1   *(Drawing a knife.)* When he comes back, grab his arms behind his back, and I'll put this in his guts. Mind he puts the wine down first – we don't want him to drop it.

PARDONER   The other drunken lout soon got hold of a loaf and a couple of bottles…

Rioter 3 *appears at the far end of stage with these. He stops to think.*

but greed knows no bounds, and he had plans of his own.

The *Apothecary* *enters holding a board as a counter. Rioter 3* *goes to the* *Apothecary* *and raps on the board.*

APOTHECARY   Yes!

RIOTER 3   Rats. I've got rats as big as wolfhounds in my barn, and they're greatly diminishing my hitherto considerable flock of chickens.

(Pause.)

APOTHECARY   Yes?

RIOTER 3   I need some poison… for the rats.

APOTHECARY   Ah! Poison. Try this *(Takes a phial of poison out of his pocket.)* It'll set fire to their insides and send smoke out of their ears.

RIOTER 3   That'll do fine.

He slaps some gold coins on the counter and leaves.

PARDONER   *(Narrating the action as it happens, slowly, allowing time for all the movements in measured mime.)* And so the youngster poured the poison into the bottles, returned to his so-called friends, greeted them cheerfully, set down the wine, ... and was foully and treacherously murdered...

Rioter 2 grabs Rioter 3 from behind. Rioter 1 stabs him. Blood is represented by red ribbons held in the hands of Rioter 1, which are let drop to unfurl.

...by the other two – who, to celebrate their new-found wealth, picked up the wine, pulled out the corks, and drank deeply...
...to experience
their own
agonizing
horrible
deaths.

Rioters 2 and 3 simulate exaggerated deaths, which should be horrible, melodramatic and protracted, moving to a climax of cymbals, drums, smoke and dancing Fiends, who enter and lead or drag the bodies up the ramp into Hell's mouth, and then take away the props.

PARDONER   *(Steps forward centre stage and addresses the audience.)* So... As I say... The love of money is the root of all evil, and the wages of sin are eternal damnation.

He holds out his money bag.

If you wish to be saved, come forward and drop gold in this bag.

The Host enters, impatient and angry.

HOST   I don't know how you've got the nerve, you bare-faced hypocrite. If you had anything to cut off, I'd cut them off, have them pickled in a jar and presented as acorns from the Garden of Gethsemane.

PARDONER *(Fearfully mincing off with **Host** in pursuit.)* Well I know when I'm not being appreciated.

SCHOLAR It seems that quite a number of people employed by the church were hell-bent on making money.

CHAUCER I couldn't possibly comment... But see for yourself when the Friar tells his tale.

*The **Friar** enters and walks across the stage. A **Serving Wench** enters opposite. The **Friar** goes to chat her up.*

THE FRIAR'S TALE

SCHOLAR Isn't he a holy man?

CHAUCER Does he look like one? Oh, he's supposed to be, all right. He's supposed to live in poverty and give up any thought of sex...

*The **Friar** and **Wench** leave, embracing. Giggles from them, off.*

He has a licence to beg in this part of town and he should pray for souls. But what does he do? Spends all his time with innkeepers and friendly women. *(Calls out.)* Eh! Friar!

*The **Friar's** head appears.*

FRIAR What!

CHAUCER Come out here and tell your story.

FRIAR You know it, you tell it. I'm busy.

*He is pulled back in by the **Wench**. **Chaucer**, sighing and shaking his head, comes forward. The **Scholar** retires to his chair.*

CHAUCER   To begin with, there was an Archdeacon, a top man in the local church, who came down heavily on thieves, fraudsters, adulterers and slanderers – provided they could pay heavy fines.

He moves to the side of stage to relate the rest of the tale. The Archdeacon enters and kneels to pray. A Summoner enters and stands before him.

A Summoner did his dirty work for him – a Summoner with a network of spies who used to point the finger at sinners, and who then collected the fines. Mainly to increase the Archdeacon's wealth, but also his own.

ARCHDEACON   *(Getting up.)* Sin! Sin! Sin!

The Summoner punctuates each 'sin' by throwing a bag of coins down in front of the Archdeacon.

SUMMONER   There's a lot of it about.

ARCHDEACON   *(Pointing at the bags.)* But more than that, surely.

He moves towards the Summoner.

Hand over the rest, you lousy thief!

He holds the Summoner by the collar.

SUMMONER   *(Slyly.)* I have expenses – which the Bishop wouldn't want to know about.

The Archdeacon, grumbling, lets him go.

I must go. No rest for the wicked. There's an old woman I need to accuse of... *(Pause.)* something, ... *(Loudly.)* and I might even catch that old goat the friar at it.

FRIAR   *(Shouting from offstage.)* You have no power to arrest me. I've got a licence.

Exit Archdeacon. Summoner sets off on his travels. The Fiends leave the scaffold and come down onto the stage. Once again they become trees, with branches held out.

CHAUCER So off he went to trap some poor old woman for a crime she didn't commit. On his walk through the woods, he caught sight of a Yeoman, a fellow-traveller.

*Enter **Yeoman**. **Yeoman** and **Summoner** walk around in circles, with **Summoner** eventually catching up.*

Always being one to make new contacts and extend his network of spies…

SUMMONER *(From close behind the **Yeoman**.)* Hello! Are you going my way?

YEOMAN *(Turning.)* I'm going this way, certainly. What's your business?

SUMMONER Just off to collect some rent that's overdue.

YEOMAN Ah, you're a bailiff, then, like me?

SUMMONER Er… Yes.

They walk in a purposeful circle as they talk.

YEOMAN Lord bless you…

CHAUCER Said the Yeoman…

YEOMAN You're a brother;
You are a bailiff and I am another!
I'd like, as I'm a stranger in these woods,
To get to know you. And, afterwards,
Become your friend if I'm so bold,
There's silver in my coffers, and some gold.
If you so happen to visit my shire
It's all yours. Just as much as you desire.

They stop and shake hands.

My friend, I live far in the north countray,
Where I shall hope to see you one fine day.

They walk.

SUMMONER   Well, since we're friends and in the same line of business, perhaps you can help me. Can you suggest any dodge, or little trick, that might help me make more of a profit? I don't care how sinful it is.

*They stop. The **Yeoman** looks deep into the **Summoner's** eyes.*

YEOMAN   My wages are low. I am poorly paid and my master is a hard man. I get what I can, any way I can. That's all I will say.

SUMMONER   *(A little overawed, but doggedly persistent.)* Come, now. I'll try my hand at anything. I don't have any scruples. I have to live, so I'll stoop to anything. I have no conscience, not at all. I'm lucky to have met you. What's your name?

*Three **Fiends** enter and stand behind the **Summoner**. One of them crouches.*

YEOMAN   *(Smiling.)* My friend. Do you want me to tell? I'm a fiend; my dwelling is in Hell.

*He pushes the **Summoner** to sit on the crouching body of a **Fiend**. Other **Fiends** hold the **Summoner**. The **Yeoman** stands over him threateningly.*

And I am here to line my pockets as best I can, as you are, and I'd go to the world's end and back to get my prey.

SUMMONER   *(Gulping.)* But you're in human form. Don't you have any fixed shape in Hell?

YEOMAN   No, indeed, we have none. We can turn ourselves into any kind of shape: sometimes like a man, or like an ape. We will become anything at all to capture souls, and we work hard at it.

SUMMONER   Why work so hard?

YEOMAN   It's because, sometimes, we're God's instruments

And carry out his commandments,
In a variety of ways and shapes and forms.
We have no power without him, and he sometimes
allows us to torture the body of a man...

*Another **Fiend** squeezes the **Summoner's** head.*

...and at other times to torment his soul.

*He looks deep into the **Summoner's** eyes again, then kisses him on the forehead before helping him up. The **Fiends** return to the scaffold.*

But let's move on. I'd like to travel with you before you part with me.

SUMMONER   Never! I'll never part with you. You are my brother and we will share everything. Whatever you earn and whatever I earn – straight down the middle. You agree?

YEOMAN   Agreed. You have my word.

They continue their circular walk.

CHAUCER   And so they walked on, until they came upon a carter...

*Two **horses** – actors with horses' masks – pull on a handcart. The **Carter** is sitting on the cart, wielding a whip.*

...who'd had a hard day and was stuck in the mud.

CARTER   *(Using whip, but tired.)* Move, damn you, move. After a day like I've had! Move or the devil take all of you, and this! *(Uses whip.)*

SUMMONER   *(Stopping to watch, with the **Yeoman**.)* Do you hear what this fellow is saying. He wants you to take everything. Come on, it's all yours.

YEOMAN   No, wait. That's not what he means at all. Hold on a minute, you'll see.

*The **Carter** gets off the cart and goes to the **horses**, pulling their heads forward.*

CARTER   May Christ bless you all. Come now. Pull.

They move forward.

That's my boys. Thanks to God. We're on our way.

*The **horses** pull the cart and **Carter** off.*

YEOMAN   See, you have to be careful. You can't trust anyone *(Pause.)* ...trust me! People like him say one thing but mean another. There's nothing for us here. Let's move on.

They continue their circular walk.

SUMMONER   A shame. But we'll make up for it. I'm on my way to see an old biddy who lives not far from here, and I'll be damned if I don't squeeze some money out of her. But she's crafty and tight-fisted. Never puts a foot wrong – but I'll think of something.

*The **Old Woman** enters and holds up board to represent a door. The **Summoner** and the **Yeoman** arrive there, and the **Summoner** knocks on the board.*

SUMMONER   Come on, you old trout, open up.

OLD WOMAN   What is it?

SUMMONER   Open the door. I'm the Summoner sent by the Archdeacon, and he wants to see you.

OLD WOMAN   I can't come, I've got a bad back.

SUMMONER   You have to. You have to answer... certain charges.

OLD WOMAN   Like what?

SUMMONER   Whatever you've been up to.

OLD WOMAN   Mm?

SUMMONER   Adultery.

OLD WOMAN   *(Shrieks with laughter.)* At my age? I've forgotten how.

SUMMONER	Poaching.
OLD WOMAN	Rubbish!
SUMMONER	Witchcraft.
OLD WOMAN	I'm no witch and you know it.
SUMMONER	You know what they do to witches, and how easily they can prove it. But I'll forget about it and walk away if you give me twelve pence.
OLD WOMAN	*(Puts down board and steps forward.)* You fool. You've picked the wrong woman. Christ is my salvation. I've done nothing wrong, and I live in holy poverty. I haven't got one penny, let alone twelve.
SUMMONER	Then give me something else. *(Points to a frying pan propped at the side of the stage.)* That frying pan. It's new. Give me that.
OLD WOMAN	I'll give it to you, all right.

*She picks it up and advances on the **Summoner**, swinging it.*

To hell with you! *(The **Summoner** falls to the floor and she hits him with the frying pan.)* The devil can take the frying pan *(Throws it down at him.)* and the devil can take you, too, if you don't repent for what you've said.

YEOMAN	Do you mean what you say?
OLD WOMAN	Of course. He can go to Hell – that's where he belongs.
YEOMAN	*(To **Summoner**.)* And do you say sorry to her?
SUMMONER	To that old bat? I'm damned if I do.
YEOMAN	And you're damned if you don't.

***Fiends** enter stage holding a long black cloth between them. The **Yeoman** picks up the pan and* *speaks triumphantly.*

This pan and you are ours by right,
We'll carry you to Hell tonight!

*The **Fiends** move forward and wrap the **Summoner**, who is now kneeling, in the cloth, before dragging him away in it, as they sing/chant.*

FIENDS   We are fiends! We come from Hell!
We'll drag the Summoner there as well!
Wrap him up in Satan's gown.
The devil's fires will burn him brown.

*He is taken off through Hell's mouth in a crescendo of music, smoke and flames. The **Yeoman-fiend** turns one last time to the audience, arms raised, as delighted as a pantomime villain. He exits.*

***Chaucer** steps forward.*

CHAUCER   Friar! *(No answer.)* Friar!

FRIAR   *(Off.)* What?

CHAUCER   We've had your story, now what's your moral?

*The **Friar** enters, adjusting his dress.*

FRIAR   Why, that summoners mend their wicked ways, repent, or be damned to Hell, of course.

***Chaucer** looks knowingly at the **Scholar**, who steps forward.*

YEOMAN   *(Bounding on and hailing the **Friar**.)* Greetings, friend. You look in need of a drink. Let me buy you one. *(Puts his arm around the **Friar**, ushering him off stage.)*

FRIAR   I'm always happy to accept a drink from a good Christian like yourself. *(Exit **Friar** and **Yeoman**.)*

Pause.

SCHOLAR   Was there anyone on your pilgrimage that it's possible to like?

CHAUCER　We had a parson who was a very good man – but rather dull. The Miller wasn't too bad a chap. A villain of sorts. Dishonest, like all millers, of course, but larger than life, hearty and fun. He was very good at wrestling, it seems, and he had a rather odd party trick of head-butting oak doors and knocking them off their hinges. He did it for us once, in a tavern just outside Faversham.

SCHOLAR　I'm sure he must have suffered brain damage.

CHAUCER　Probably, but he was good to have around. Always telling jokes. Quite good ones. Hated carpenters for some reason. We had a reeve with us who was a carpenter. They were always at each other's throats. It might be interesting for you to hear both their tales. But be prepared to be offended.

Come on, Miller! Leave your boozing and give us your story.

THE MILLER'S TALE

*The **Miller** enters and takes centre stage. **Chaucer** and **Scholar** retire to chairs.*

MILLER　I'm somewhat drunk. But don't blame me, blame the beer. My story's about a carpenter, an old man who was stupid enough to marry a girl called Alison who was much younger than he. And what a girl she was, (*Alison* enters and wiggles for his delight.) as slim and supple as a weasel; lively, frisky and skittish. Her mouth was sweet as mead, or ale and honey. What a peach – fit for a king. But the Carpenter was keen to keep her for himself, and kept her closely confined in the house. A bit like having a young colt firmly tied to a stake. She wasn't going to settle for that, and the idiot went and made it easy for her. He took in a student from Oxford University as a lodger…

*Nicholas enters. **Alison** and **Nicholas** flirt outrageously, circling each other and grinning.*

…and you know how randy students can be. To the Carpenter, who was a nitwit, Nicholas the student was a model guest. He often stayed in his room and read his books on astrology. But one day, when the Carpenter was busy at work, he made his intentions plain.

*The **Miller** moves to one side. **Nicholas** grabs **Alison** by the buttocks. She slaps him and he falls.*

NICHOLAS   Oh, Alison. I am sick with love for you. If my desire is not requited, I will surely die.

ALISON   You keep your grubby little hands to yourself, you lecher, or I'll scream for my husband.

NICHOLAS   You can't prefer him to me, surely. He's old, he's ugly and he's stupid. He's a carpenter, for goodness' sake.

ALISON   *(After a moment's thought.)* You're right. But he's also got a bad temper and a big… set of tools.

NICHOLAS   Well, I'm hardly going to seduce you in front of him.

ALISON   I should think not. But if I am going to give in to your irresistible charm, you'd better make sure that no-one, least of all my husband, finds out.

NICHOLAS   You mean… you're going to accept me? *(He stands up.)*

ALISON   Provided my husband doesn't get to know, I'll take all that you've got.

MILLER   So off trotted Nicholas to plot.

*Exit **Nicholas**.*

But Nicholas wasn't Alison's only admirer.

*Enter **Absolon**, who cuts a bizarre figure. He wears*

*brightly-coloured clothes and has long, curly, fan-shaped hair. He eyes up **Alison**. She kneels to pray.*

Absolon. A curious chap. His hair was curly and gold and shaped like a fan. He dressed… flamboyantly, and had many talents. He could shave and cut hair. He helped out in the church, could dance a jig, sing *(**Absolon** does so in a very high falsetto.)* and play the guitar. A man of many parts… but very squeamish about farting.

ABSOLON   Oh, Alison, you gorgeous creature. How I love you, how I desire you, how I ache for you.

***Alison** exits.*

MILLER   Often, he would stand beneath her bedroom window, sing and strum the guitar. *(Does just this whilst **Nicholas** and **Alison** enter together. **Absolon** leaves.)* Nicholas had been thinking…

NICHOLAS   Alison, I'm taking food and drink to my room to last for a few days. If your husband asks for me, say you haven't seen me.

***Nicholas** exits and goes to bedroom station. **Carpenter** enters.*

CARPENTER   Where's Nicholas?

ALISON   I haven't seen him. *(Exits.)*

MILLER   The Carpenter was stupid enough to worry about Nick, and went to his room. *(Actions follow narration.)* He banged on the door. *(**Nicholas** is sitting up on the 'bed', staring into space.)* No answer… He banged again… Then he looked through the keyhole, and saw…
Nicholas…
Bolt upright in bed…
Staring into space…
With an amazed look on his face…
So…
He broke down the door, rushed to Nicholas, and

patted his face, saying:

CARPENTER Nicholas, what's the matter? Speak to me. I knew it would come to no good. It doesn't pay to read books about astronomy, astrology and *(Pointing to books beside the bed.)* …adjamathology. No-one can pry into God's works and survive… So, tell me, what have you found out?

NICHOLAS *(Coming to.)* Fetch me a drink and I'll tell you everything.

*The **Carpenter** snatches a bottle off the shelf and offers it.*

Listen and say nothing. Last night, I was studying my books and I heard a voice. I swear it was the voice of our Lord, Jesus Christ. He was warning me and he said this:

That on Monday next, at about nine at night,
there'll be a fall of rain – so fierce a spate.
Even Noah's flood was never half so great.
This world, said he, in less time than an hour.
Must all be drowned, so frightful the downpour.
Thus all mankind must drown and wholly perish.

CARPENTER What? Alas! Alack!

*The **Carpenter** backs away after listening intently, and almost falls downstairs.*

Must my poor wife drown? Alison, my love?

MILLER The fool was so overcome he almost fell.

CARPENTER Is there no hope? No way out of this?

MILLER This, of course, was exactly what Nicholas planned.

NICHOLAS Yes, there is, if you listen to the right kind of advice and don't try to act alone. Haven't you heard how the Lord spoke to Noah and saved him by telling him to build the ark? *(The **Carpenter** nods.)* Then listen.

> *Nicholas mimes expressively whilst the **Carpenter** listens in awestruck silence and occasionally nods.*

MILLER Nicholas told the old oaf that speed was vital. He ordered him to fetch into the house three tubs or half-barrels: one for each of them. They had to be large, able to float and to contain one day's food and drink. Then, he must hang them in the rafters from ropes. When the water comes high enough in the night, the tubs will be able to float. Each one is to have an axe to cut the rope and float away.

NICHOLAS ...Then we'll be as happy as ducks, paddling about. We'll be able to shout 'Hi! Good morning!' And for the rest of our lives we'll be lords of the world. But a word of warning. God commands that there be no noise or talking. Nor must there be any naughty stuff between Alison and you. In fact, I must go in the tub that hangs between you, to stop you getting frisky. No more words. You must go away and prepare for the night.

MILLER *(Throughout the **Miller's** speech, the **Carpenter** gathers and assembles his equipment with the help of the **Fiends**. The tubs can be two-dimensional cutouts, attached to ropes and hung from the Hell's mouth scaffold.)* Imagination can work powerfully on people. The Carpenter could see his lovely Alison drowning, and so began to shake with emotion. But he pulled himself together...
Found three tubs...
Hung them from the rafters with ropes... *(Held by **Fiends** standing on top of Hell's mouth.)*
Put steps between them...
Stocked them with axes, cheese and bread...
Shut all the doors and got ready for bed...

> *Alison and **Nicholas** and the **Carpenter** act out the **Miller's** narrative.*

When everything was as it should be

They climbed in to sleep, all three.
The carpenter, after his busy day
Fell dead asleep, round curfew time, I'd say.

Pause.

Alison and Nick got up and softly sped
For fun and frolics in the marital bed.

They run to the bedroom.

Meanwhile…

Absolon *enters.*

…the lovelorn Absolon had heard the Carpenter
had gone to work away from home and left the
gorgeous Alison alone.

ABSOLON Oh verily I am filled with great delight.
I'm sure to have some sexy fun tonight.
I'll stand beside the window in the wall.
And tell Alison I love her once and all.
And what is more, I don't intend to miss
The chance of giving her at least a little kiss.

He moves to the bedroom window and coughs.

Where are you my honey, my sweet Alison? My
pretty chick, awake. It is your darling Absolon,
desperate for love of you. Come to the window and
give me a kiss.

ALISON Get away from the window, you jackanapes. *(Sitting
up in bed.)* I wouldn't dream of kissing you. I love
someone else. Get away or I'll throw something at
you. Go on, get lost and let me sleep.

ABSOLON Oh woe, woe! Oh woe is me! Was ever a lover so
abused? All I desire is one kiss from your sweet
cherry lips.

ALISON Oh for goodness sake. Will you go away if I just
give you one little kiss?

ABSOLON   Yes, of course, sweetheart.

ALISON   All right, get ready. *(To **Nicholas**.)* Keep quiet and I'll give you a laugh. Wait and see.

She gets out of bed and holds a false bottom or pink cushion to her rump.

ABSOLON   *(On his knees.)* I'm in for a treat. I'm going to make the most of this, and who knows what might follow after. *(Prepares himself.)*

MILLER   *(As **Alison** mimes with the aid of her suitably-shaped prop, which **Absolon** kisses enthusiastically.)*
Derk was the night as pitch, or as the cole,
And at the window out she putte hir hole,
And Absolon, him fil no bet ne wers,
But with his mouth he kiste hir naked ers
Full savourly, er he were war of this.
Abak he stirte, and thoughte it was amis,
For wel he wiste a womman hath no berd.
He felt a thing al rough and long yherd.

ABSOLON   What was that? Alison doesn't have a beard.

Truth dawns.

Oh my good lord! Bleurgh!

*He mimes to the **Miller's** commentary.*

MILLER   *(Loving this.)* He rubbed his lips with sand, straw, cloth, sawdust and wood chippings. From now on, he was cured of his lovesickness. He vowed revenge, and went to visit his friend, Gervaise, a blacksmith.

Absolon *goes over to Hell's mouth.* ***Gervaise*** *appears with a red-hot plough coulter.*

ABSOLON   What oh, Gervaise!

GERVAISE   Absolon. What are you doing up at this hour? Chasing skirt and being made a fool of, I'll guess. What can I do for you?

ABSOLON   A favour. I need… something.

GERVAISE   Go on.

ABSOLON   *(Decides, and points to the glowing implement.)* Can I borrow that coulter? That'll do.

GERVAISE   What on earth do you want with this?

ABSOLON   Be that as it may.
I'll tell you – but on another day.

He takes the coulter and returns to the window.

Pretty bird! Alison! I liked that so much that I've come for another. And I have a present for you in return for a kiss.

MILLER   *(Narrating while **Nicholas** acts out the scene.)*
This Nicholas was risen for to pisse,
And thoughte he wolde amenden al the jape;
He sholde kisse his ers er that he scape.
And up the windowe dide he hastily,
And out his ers he putteth prively
Over the buttok, to the haunche-bon; *(**Nicholas** does so, using **Alison's** prop.)*
And therewith spak this clerk, this Absolon.

ABSOLON   Speak, sweet bird, I know not where you art.

MILLER   This Nicholas anon let flee a fart, *(Musical effect.)*
As greet as it had been a thonder-dent,
That with the strook he was almoost yblent;
and he was redy with his iren hoot,
And Nicholas amidde the ers he smoot. *(**Absolon** jabs **Nicholas** in the buttocks with the red hot coulter.)*

NICHOLAS   *(Screaming.)* Help, water! Water! Help, for God's sake!

*He runs to sit on the chamber pot, still shouting 'Water, water'. **Alison** runs to help.*

MILLER   *(As the mime takes place.)* At the cry of water, the

Carpenter woke up suddenly, thinking it was the flood. He grabbed his axe...
Cut the rope...
And fell twenty feet into the street, *(The Carpenter topples from behind his barrel.)* breaking his arm, much to the amusement of his neighbours.

All freeze in tableau. Chaucer and Scholar come forward. Fiends and cast gather round and laugh. Percussion accompanies fall.

CHAUCER So, Miller, what's the point of your story?

SCHOLAR Yes. You obviously think it's funny to see people cheated, tricked, battered, broken and burned!

MILLER *(To audience.)* Thus swived was this carpenter's wyf,
For al his keping and his jalousie;
And Absolon hath kist hir nether ye;
And Nicholas is scalded in the towte.
This tale is doon, and God save al the route!

Triumphantly leads off the company, except for Chaucer and the Scholar.

SCHOLAR He doesn't like carpenters does he? And wasn't there a carpenter among your company, you say?

CHAUCER There was; who swore revenge for the insult. You shall see how, shortly. But for now I'm tired, and in need of refreshment. Time for a break. *(Exeunt.)*

Fade to black.

END OF ACT ONE

ACT TWO

THE REEVE'S TALE

Host enters.

HOST Well, ladies and gentlemen, here we are in Deptford.

*The **Reeve** enters.*

So it's high time you told your tale, Reeve. Out with it.

*Exit **Host**.*

REEVE *(To audience.)* This drunken Miller has just told us about the diddling of a carpenter. As I'm one, I'm sure he did it to scoff at me. So, I'm going to indulge in a bit of tit for tat. I'll use his own language, lout that he is; I hope he goes and breaks his bloody neck.

*Enter **Simkin**.*

In Trumpington, near Cambridge,
There's a stream which has a bridge,
And by this bridge is a mill.
In it lived a miller.

***Simkin** stands in position, other characters follow.*

He was as proud as a peacock,
Strong as an ox,
Good at wrestling and knocking doors off hinges
With his head!
And what a head it was –
Heavy, flat-nosed, drooling,
Like an ape.
Nobody dared cross him
Or he'd threaten them.
But he was the biggest villain –
He stole corn and meal from his customers

Like all millers.
This one was called 'Show-off Simkin'.
And he had a wife... *(Enter **Wife**.)*
...Who was very, very stuck up and superior.
Simkin wouldn't take on just anybody.
She had to have a good dowry,
Be well brought-up, and a maid.
This one was the daughter of a parson. *(**Wife** links arms with **Simkin** and they strut up and down.)*
What a sight they were together,
Strutting about at church.
Everyone had to call her Madam
And treat her like royalty.
If anyone flirted with her
Or made a pass... *(A **Fiend** pinches the **Wife's** bottom. **Simkin** chases it away.)*
...Simkin would be after them with his knife.
*(**Daughter** enters.)*
They had a daughter,
A girl of twenty
With a pug nose,
Glassy eyes,
Big buttocks and bosom.
Lovely hair, though.
The local priest was going to leave her all his money,
Provided she kept her maidenhood
Until she married into a good family.
Oh, and they had a baby. *(The baby – a doll – is thrown to the **Wife** from off stage.)*

*The family move into position; **Simkin** goes to turn the wheel of the upturned cart, the **Wife** and **Daughter** dust and sweep.*

Simkin used to grind the corn for a college in Cambridge.
But he used to steal a good fraction of it.
Two students, called Alan and John... *(They enter,*

*with a **Horse** loaded with a large sack.)*
...Offered to take the corn,
And make sure he didn't steal any of it.

SIMKIN Morning, Alan; morning, John.

ALAN Hello, Simkin, you old scoundrel.

JOHN *(Tying up the **Horse**, or asking a member of the audience to hold the rope.)* Here's the corn from the college, and we've come to grind it. *(Gives sack to **Simkin**.)*

SIMKIN Away with you, I'm the one who'll do the grinding.

ALAN If you must. And we'll watch you do it.

***Wife** and **Daughter** leave.*

SIMKIN *(To audience.)* Who do they think they are! These hoity toity, arty-farty, wishy-washy students think they're too clever to be fooled. Well, sure they can. Instead of giving flour, I'll give them bran.
And, meanwhile, I'll give their horse a run
Off to the wild mares, to have some fun.

*He releases the **Horse** and slaps its flanks. The **Horse** runs off with an enthusiastic whinny. **Simkin** returns to grind corn. The 'mill' can be a wheel of the cart, tipped on its side.*

ALAN *(Goes to find **Horse**.)* Hey, John, look here, our horse has gone. Where is he?

REEVE And so the students forgot their plan to keep an eye on things.

WIFE *(Enters running.)* You fools, you didn't tie him up properly. He's gone off running towards the fens.

***Alan** and **John** run off to find **Horse**.*

SIMKIN Fools is right. They thought they could put one over on me because they're students, but I'll have the last laugh. Here's some of their flour. Bake a nice big cake for us.

Alan and *John* run back in, chasing **Horse**, who is finally caught.

ALAN   Oh hell, hell, hell. That's ruined everything. The miller's pinched the corn, we're exhausted, it's getting to be night time and it's too late to travel back to college.

JOHN   Here, Simkin, we're hungry, tired and it's getting late. For God's love and mercy, would you agree to put us up for the night?

SIMKIN   Well it's a small, humble place, to be sure – unless you fancy scholars can make it bigger with your disputations and your rhetoric.

JOHN   All we ask is for food, drink and a bed. We'll pay – cash on the nail.

SIMKIN   *(Magnanimous.)* My house is your house. Have ale, bread, *(Tankards and bread are brought by* **Wife** *and* **Daughter**.*)* and we'll put up another bed in our bedroom.

Fiends do this: they bring on two beds, each of which consists of a blanket stretched across two posts. A cradle is positioned next to the bed of **Simkin** and his **Wife**. She puts the baby into it.

REEVE   *(As mime takes place.)* And so they made a party of it. The miller, flushed with success, had several drinks too many. He was hiccupping and talking through his nose and croaking as though he had a bad cold. So off he went to bed, and his wife was in nearly as bad a state as he was. She set the baby's cradle by her bed, so that she might rock it to sleep, if need be...
And the Daughter went to bed... *(Wooden ramp, in bedroom.)*
And Alan...
And John...

*They all do so. **Alan** and **John** in one upright bed, **Simkin** and his **Wife** in the other, the **Daughter** in the bedroom.*

Simkin had had a skinful, that's for sure. He started honking from both ends, and his wife joined in the chorus. *(Suitable snoring and farting noises, musical effects.)* Alan, hearing this music, nudged John.

ALAN Are you awake? Did you ever hear such a song as these two, at their evening prayer. I shan't get any sleep, I tell you. But maybe it's all for the best, for I aim to get even with that thief. He stole our corn and I'm going to get some kind of recompense.

JOHN What do you mean?

ALAN I'm going to pay him back by sleeping with his daughter.

JOHN What? You're mad. If he catches you, he'll kill you.

ALAN Nonsense. He couldn't hurt a fly.

REEVE And so Alan tiptoed to the daughter's bed. *(He does so, and gets under the sheet with her.)* Before she knew it, he was under way and it was too late for her to make a fuss. In fact, she fell in love with him instantly. John was jealous.

JOHN Well, he's having a good time and I'm lying here like a mug. Still, if I get half a chance…

REEVE Before too long, the miller's worthy wife staggered out of bed to answer the call of nature. *(**Wife** does so – off stage.)* It was dark and she was drunk, but John saw his chance.

JOHN Nothing ventured, nothing gained.

He tiptoes out of bed and moves the cradle over beside him.

REEVE So, when the wife returned…

*She staggers in with her arms outstretched to feel her way. She goes to **Simkin's** bed but can't find the cradle. Stumbles around until...*

WIFE Oops, silly me – nearly got in bed with the students. That would never do. Here's my darling diddums. *(Finds cradle – gets in bed with **John**, who grabs her.)* Ooh-er! *(And other suitable noises.)*

REEVE Four out of the five had the night of their lives and worked hard at it until cock crow. *(Two beds show signs of activity. After a while, a cock crows.)*

ALAN It's morning and I'm getting tired. I must leave you darling Molly.

DAUGHTER Oh my dearest, so be it. But before you leave to go back to college, go to the larder by the back door and there you'll find a cake made from the flour that my father stole from you. Take it with you.

ALAN Thank you, my angel, I will. Now, before it gets too late, I must slip back in bed beside my mate.

*He leaves the **Daughter's** bed and gropes his way. Finding the cradle, he avoids the bed next to it, and gets into bed with **Simkin**.*

(Whispering.) It was great. That Molly was lovely. She kept me happy all night. I've never had a better time.

SIMKIN *(Starts up.)* Oh you haven't, have you? You've dishonoured my daughter, born of noble blood. I'll have your tripes for this.

REEVE *(Accompanied by mime of fight.)*
Simkin grabbed Alan by the Adam's apple.
And he, in defence, began a heated grapple.
He gave the show-off Simkin a bloody nose.
He groaned and woke the wife up from her doze.
She hadn't realised what went on that night,
And thought the students had begun to fight.

She grabbed a stick that was lying by the bed
And, unaware, smashed her husband on the head.
The students saw that it was time to scram,
Grabbed cake and horse, and out the door they ran.
(All the actions complete by this point.)
So that's how the thieving miller got well beat
And soundly punished for being such a cheat.
His wife and daughter tumbled in delight,
The students truly had a cheerful night.
God save you all and keep you, so say I,
And learn to do as you would be done by.

Exeunt all. **Fiends** *move the cart to an upright position downstage.* **Chaucer** *and the* **Scholar** *come forward.*

THE WIFE OF BATH'S TALE

SCHOLAR Men! Obsessed with petty rivalries, sneaky tricks and sex. They never grow up.

CHAUCER Ah! You should hear the Wife of Bath on the subject. Not that she didn't like men. She'd been married to five of them and there had been a number of other… friendships. She got to be something of an expert on how to treat men.

SCHOLAR Five husbands!

Wife of Bath enters. She flirts with members of the audience at every opportunity.

WIFE OF BATH They had a habit of dying on me. And I wasn't one to go without for any length of time. Roll on the sixth, that's what I say. Mind you, the sex wasn't all that important to me. It's just something to keep a man happy – part of the bargain. I give him what he wants, and he gives me what I want.

SCHOLAR What do you want?

CHAUCER What does any woman want?

SCHOLAR Love and affection?

WIFE OF BATH Love and affection don't pay bills.

SCHOLAR Money?

WIFE OF BATH Well – that goes without saying. I don't want to starve; I want to be comfortably off. But it's more than that. Women must be allowed to do as they please, and not be treated as slaves. You heard that numbskull of a Miller and the idiot Reeve: there were two kinds of men in their stories – those that wanted to keep their women locked away like treasured possessions, and those that just wanted their wicked way with them. Frankly, I have more sympathy with the latter. I can't abide men who refuse women freedom.

SCHOLAR Did your husbands do that?

WIFE OF BATH Of the five, three of them were good and two were bad. The best were the old ones. They signed over their property, and I kept them busy chasing me around. The fifth, though, I married for love, and spent a long time regretting it. He was a scholar, and read all kinds of garbage. In particular, he was always reading the work of Valerius – a writer who hated women, advised against marriage and listed all the dreadful things that women were supposed to have done. He kept reading bits out to me – so-called words of wisdom, like 'Better to live with a lion or a dragon than take up with a scolding woman,' or 'A pretty woman, if she isn't chaste, is like a gold ring stuck in a sow's nose.' Poppycock!

Husband enters, reading.

One night, he was reading this damned book, and I got so angry I ripped some pages out of it and gave him a fist in the face. *(This is acted out.)* He gave me a slap round the head – which is the reason I'm deaf in one ear. *(She falls and groans on the floor.)*

You've murdered me, you thief, just to get at my land. You've murdered me, but I'll give you one last kiss before I die.

HUSBAND Darling sweetheart, forgive me. I'll never hit you again, I promise. Please forgive me. *(He bends to kiss her.)*

WIFE OF BATH Swine. Take that! *(Hits him.)* I can't say any more, I'm nearly dead.

HUSBAND Please don't leave me. I'll be a good boy from now on.

WIFE OF BATH Well, burn your book. *(He throws it through Hell's mouth. **Wife of Bath** instantly leaps up, a new woman.)* And we'll hear no more of that rubbish. In future, I'll run the household. You have to put trust in me.

HUSBAND Sweetheart, my own true faithful wife,
Do as you please from now, all your life:
Guard your honour and look after my estate.

WIFE OF BATH And that, then, was the end of the debate.

*Exit **Husband**.*

Men need putting firmly in their place
And sometimes require a smack across the face.
I see some men among you have turned pale;
It's high time, then, that I began my tale.
It is set in the olden days, the days of King Arthur,
Which were also the days of elves, fairies and magic.
One day, one of Arthur's knights,
Who wasn't the brightest creature ever to grace the round table…

*The **Wife** moves to side of the stage. A **Knight** enters, followed by a **Girl**.*

…was idling by the riverbank when he saw a girl, got a rush of blood to the head, couldn't resist his instincts, and went for her.

*The **Knight** grabs the **Girl** and carries her to the cart, where he attempts to fondle her. She kicks him. The **Knight** is left much the worse for wear. The **Girl** runs for help and returns with **King**, **Queen**, **knights** and **ladies**.*

GIRL   *(Points to **Knight**.)* There he is – he tried to take my honour.

KING   I will not have this outrageous behaviour occurring among my knights. We are supposed to be the souls of chivalry. Arrest him. *(**Knights** do so.)* And for this foul crime, I decree that you will be beheaded!

*The crowd react, shocked: the **ladies** quite like the **Knight**. But one of the **Fiends** comes forward with an axe.*

QUEEN   Arthur, my dear. Don't you think that's a teeny-weeny little bit steep?

*Other **ladies** murmur agreement.*

KING   Perhaps. But I won't have chumps like this going round molesting innocent women.

QUEEN   Well, teach him a lesson, then. Let's rehabilitate him. Chopping his head off seems somewhat drastic.

KING   Mm. Very well. What do you suggest?

QUEEN   A task. Send him on a quest. If he can find the answer to a riddle within the next twelve months, then he will be spared. If not, he gets the chop.
Listen here, you:
Your fate is still in the balance.
You have a year's grace.
Travel the world if necessary to answer this question: *(Expectant pause.)* what is the thing that women most desire? Return here in one year, with or without the answer. You must give your pledge.

*The **Knight** agrees and kneels. He is released. **Fiend** with axe departs disappointed.*

WIFE OF BATH He wasn't happy, but he didn't have much choice. He didn't know the answer straight off, so he set off on his travels *(The **Knight** goes on a circular walk around the stage.)* and asked everyone he met. In fact, the poor thing must have got sick of asking it.

*The **Knight** takes out a scroll with the question printed on it. The **cast** disperse around the stage and offer their suggestions. Alternatively, the **Fiends** could interview members of the audience and call out the suggestions: 'Money', 'Honour', 'Fine clothes', 'Happiness', 'A bit of how's your father', 'Compliments'.*

WIFE OF BATH Now that's not far from the truth. We all like a bit of flattery.

Offered answers continue: 'Their own way', 'To make a fuss', 'To be thought trustworthy and discreet'.

Interesting answer. Women are good to confide in, and it's said they don't spread stories around, however difficult it may be. But it's nonsense! Women can never keep anything secret.

*She beckons members of the cast over. They sit to listen. The **Knight** listens from a distance with growing impatience.*

Take the wife of King Midas, for instance. The King, if you'll remember, was cursed with a pair of donkey's ears. He kept them hidden most of the time, but his wife knew, of course, and he begged her never to tell a soul. She promised, but the responsibility pressed heavily on her. Finally she could stand it no longer, and ran to a lake near her home, dipped her head beneath the water, and said 'My husband has a pair of donkey's ears', hoping no-one would find out.

KNIGHT   Can we get on?

WIFE OF BATH   I wouldn't be in such a hurry if I were you. *(To listening cast and audience.)* You'll have to look up the rest of that little story. Anyway, the Knight was grumpy because he couldn't come up with a satisfactory answer. *(The **Knight** continues his circular walk.)* On the day he had to return to the court, he came upon a strange and incredibly ugly old woman on a country lane.

*Enter **Old Woman**.*

OLD WOMAN   *(To **Knight**.)* You look down in the mouth, you poor soul. What's a handsome young man like you doing looking so miserable? I'd be quite happy to help you out you know, young man. I believe in being neighbourly.

KNIGHT   I don't see what you can do. I'm a dead man if I can't tell King Arthur what the thing is that women most desire. If you can help, I'd reward you well.

OLD WOMAN   That's easy, young man. I know what the Queen would say to that one, with her modern-day views. If I tell you, though, promise you'll grant me a wish as soon as the King pardons you.

KNIGHT   Of course. I'll promise anything. My life's at stake.

OLD WOMAN   Good: a nice young man like you is sure to keep his word. That's settled then. You'll be all right. This is what you have to say.

*Whispers in his ear. Exit **Old Woman**. The **Knight** does another circuit. **King**, **Queen**, **knights** and **ladies** come on stage with **Fiend/axeman**.*

WIFE OF BATH   The Knight was relieved, and walked confidently back to the royal court to give his answer. The King and Queen, lords and ladies gathered to hear him. *(They do so. **Fiend** with axe is eager.)*

QUEEN   *(To **Knight**.)* Come, then. What do you have to say?

WIFE OF BATH The Knight didn't hesitate. He was confident, and announced in ringing tones:

KNIGHT In general, your majesty, women desire most to have dominion over their husbands and lovers. They wish for mastery. I believe that's the right answer, and I put myself at your mercy.

He kneels.

QUEEN Wonderful. Absolutely right. There isn't a woman here who would argue with that.

*Everyone cheers except the **Fiend**. The **Queen** helps the **Knight** to his feet.*

OLD WOMAN *(Stepping forward.)* Good, then I must claim the Knight's promise to grant me a wish in return for the answer. I desire… that he marries me.

KNIGHT What! Oh anything but that – I'll give you all the money I have, rather than that.

OLD WOMAN Never. A curse on us both if you break your promise. I want to be your wife and one true love.

WIFE OF BATH He had to accept that this must happen and they were married speedily. It wasn't a particularly joyful occasion.

*The **Queen** brings the two together to hold hands. The **King** mouths a blessing. The **knights** and **ladies** throw confetti and then form a guard of honour. They depart, leaving only the **Knight** and **Old Woman** onstage. He paces up and down as his new wife looks on.*

In fact, he was full of misery and mourning, and hid away from her most of the time. As night loomed on the first day of his marriage, he was less than enthusiastic.

OLD WOMAN Dear husband. Bless me! Do all married knights behave like you? Is this the custom around here?

I am your own dear love and your wife,
Also the one who saved your life.
I've never wronged you, tell me what I can do to
set this right.

KNIGHT   It can never be set right. Never. You are so hideous
and old and basely born.

OLD WOMAN   Is that the reason for your distress?

KNIGHT   Of course it is. Are you surprised?

OLD WOMAN   Well, then. Let me see. All would be better if you
behaved courteously, as a knight should. It seems,
though, that you are only a knight by birth. A true
gentleman should follow Christian virtues and be
gentle both in public and in private, always being
prepared to behave well. Take any fire and place it
in the hearth of the darkest, loneliest house in the
deepest forest. Even though no-one is there to see
it, I swear it will do as a fire should, and burn until
it dies. A lord's son should do the same, not just
claim to be well-treated because of noble birth. If
he behaves like a churl, he is a churl. True nobility
comes by grace.

As for my poverty, you should know that Jesus, our
heavenly king, chose a life of poverty. Whoever is
happy and content with his or her lot should be
counted rich. Poverty, if you're humble, will often
teach you to know God.

As for my being old, it's true. But you should
respect me for my age; youth should honour the
aged.

As for my ugliness. Well, you can never suspect me
of being unfaithful. I'll give you all that you want
and there's no risk of others being interested. So
choose. You can have me old, ugly and loyal, or
beautiful, young, and with a pack of young men
hanging round me. That's the choice, what will it be?

KNIGHT *(After a thoughtful pause.)* My lady love and sweet wife. You argue well, and I place myself in your hands. You make the choice, whatever you want it to be. Whatever you choose is good enough for me.

OLD WOMAN So I have mastery over you and may decide?

KNIGHT Certainly; I'm sure it's best.

OLD WOMAN Then kiss me and don't let's argue any more. I'll be both to you – a loyal and loving wife and as pretty as a queen.

He goes to kiss her, and she takes off her mask.

WIFE OF BATH And when the Knight saw that this was so
He was bathed in joy and perfectly aglow.
He took her up in both his arms in bliss.
They kiss; a thousand, thousand times they kiss.
And she obeyed him in all things that might
Give to him satisfaction and delight.

*They retire off stage as the **Wife of Bath** takes centre stage.*

So I curse and bring down pestilence on the lives
Of those who won't be governed by their wives.

Exit.

THE NUN'S PRIEST'S TALE

Chaucer and Scholar come forward.

CHAUCER I'm sure you liked that tale better. A little more heart-warming?

SCHOLAR Yes – and we didn't have women treated like doormats, for once.

CHAUCER For once? My friends' little stories didn't always do women down. Think back over what you've heard tonight.

SCHOLAR Well…

Host enters.

CHAUCER   Still, let's try to avoid arguments and keep things on a cheerful note.

HOST   I quite agree. I'm all for liveliness and fun. Can't stand grim and gloomy tales. Least of all tedious and sermonising ones.

CHAUCER   Who's next, then? And it will have to be the last for tonight – it's close to my bedtime.

HOST   The Priest who came along with the nuns. He seems a cheery chappy. Not always on the make like the Friar and the Pardoner. And if he tells a story with a moral, he won't grind us into boredom with it.

CHAUCER   Very well. Come forward, Priest. *(The **Nun's Priest** enters.)* What's your tale about?

NUN'S PRIEST   Quite a serious topic, really – whether we have free will or whether our fates are predestined for us.

HOST   *(Groans.)* Oh, no.

Chaucer and *Scholar* resume their seats.

NUN'S PRIEST   Don't worry. It's really a jolly little fable set in the yard by a cottage owned by a hard-up widow who led a virtuous and simple life with her two daughters.

Widow and two *daughters* enter.

She was frugal and never overdid it. Wouldn't touch wine… *(**Host** is not impressed.)* and lived off bread and eggs with the occasional bit of bacon. But the true hero of the tale is her great cockerel Chantecleer…

*He enters with his flaming red comb. **Widow** and daughters leave.*

…Who she kept enclosed in the yard.

And what a bird he was.
He had a mighty crow, with which he kept the time
every fifteen minutes of the hour
He crowed out loud with all his power.
(*Chantecleer* crows.)
He had a bright red comb and jet black beak,
And overall was a burnished gold colour.
(*Chantecleer* struts around.)
He had seven hens for delectation and delight,
(**Hens** enter, cluck around and take up position on
the bedroom station.)
...To keep him happy through the day and night
And his favourite was
The gentle, kind and courteous,
Exquisitely beautiful
Lady Pertelote. (**Pertelote** appears.)
Chantecleer adored Pertelote with all his heart.
(Much primping and flaunting from **Pertelote** before
she and **Chantecleer** settle on the bedroom scaffold.)
But one night, as they slept upon their perch.
Chantecleer's troubled heart gave a lurch. (**Fiends**
attack **Chantecleer** and drag him towards Hell's
mouth.)
Trapped in a horrifying dream,
The distressed cock let out a desperate scream. (He
screams, and the **Fiends** drop him, then run off to
Hell's mouth.)

PERTELOTE   (Goes to **Chantecleer**.) What is it? What's wrong?
Tell me.

CHANTECLEER   Oh, dear. I'm still fluttering with fright. (He gets up.)
What a fearsome dream.
I dreamt that I was walking in a yard
When a creature like a dog pounced on me.
It was a kind of yellow-red colour. Its ears and tail
were tipped with black, and it had two glowing
eyes. It was going to drag me off and kill me.

PERTELOTE   What? Now you have lost all my love. I couldn't possibly be married to a coward. My husband must be generous, wise and brave, and here's you, terrified out of your wits by a paltry dream. You know what causes dreams, don't you? Overeating and flatulence. You need to purge yourself of choler and melancholy, which create wind in the system and stomach cramps. You know what your problem is, don't you?

CHANTECLEER What?

PERTELOTE Constipation. You need a good laxative. There are plenty of suitable herbs in the garden. Chew some and have a good clear-out. You'll soon be cock a doodle-doing as merrily as ever.

CHANTECLEER Thank you for your helpful advice, Madam, but I really do think that there is more to this than the state of my bowels! Many philosophers are completely convinced that dreams can foretell the future, whether it be good or bad. Cicero has a story to illustrate this:

The story can be presented in mime.

Two friends set out on a pilgrimage and eventually came to a town which was so crowded with travellers that there were no rooms left to stay in. Just for the night, the two friends had to part in order to find beds. One got a decent room in a hostel, another had to stay in a barn with farm animals. The one in the hostel had a dream as he lay in bed. It seemed his friend came to him and claimed he would die unless he received help. He shrugged it off as a nightmare, but the figure of his friend appeared again, saying he had been murdered. Sure enough, he had. The man in the hostel went to discover his friend's body in the morning. So, my Pertelote, you can see it is unwise to ignore dreams and their messages.

PERTELOTE Rubbish. Like I say: chew some licorice and sennapods. They go right through you. Once your stomach's at rest, you'll sleep soundly.

CHANTECLEER Let's forget all this depressing talk, anyway. I'll do as you say. You are my whole joy and happiness and make me forget my troubles. I will defy all visions and dreams.

NUN'S PRIEST He soon felt like a king again, and was no longer scared. He strutted around once more, master of the farmyard. (*Chantecleer* does so.) But beware the sin of pride. Happiness of this kind is so short-lived, and one day soon after, a sly black fox, who had been waiting in the woods for weeks, came to lie in wait for Chantecleer.

Fox enters to wait by ramp to Hell's mouth.

...As was predestined by divine foresight
And foretold in the dream.
He'd done as Pertelote had bid him do,
And women's advice is fatal as a rule.
Unaware of danger, he crowed loudly (*Chantecleer* does so.) as his wives took a dust bath in the sun. (*Hens* roll around on stage.)

Until
Suddenly,
In the cabbage patch
He saw the fox (*Chantecleer* does so.)
And was terror-struck!
He made to be off.

FOX Hang on, old chap, you can't be scared of me
Proud Chantecleer, it's you I've come to see.
I hear you have a powerful, vibrant crow;
I've come to hear it louder, don't you know.
Don't disappoint me, please let me hear your song.
Deep breath, eyes shut and belt it loud and long.

NUN'S PRIEST How pride comes before a drastic fall,

Chantecleer puffed up and stood strong and tall.
*(**Chantecleer** crows.)*
So Foxy leapt and grabbed him firm and good,
Slung him on his back and made off to the wood.
*(**Fox** picks up **Chantecleer**.)*
It took a little time for the hens to realise, but when
they did they raised the most enormous hullabaloo.
(All cast clucking, crowing, throwing feathers, etc.)
They alarmed the widow *(**Widow** and **Daughters***
enter.) and her daughters, the dogs, the farmers, the
workers of all kinds, *(Other members of cast enter.*
*They, the **Widow**, **Daughters**, **Pertelote** and **hens***
*chase **Fox** and **Chantecleer** around the stage.)* who
blew and hooted and screeched and flew after the
fearsome fox.

Massive hullabaloo of klaxons, horns, bugles, carried
*by cast, who do circuits of the stage. The **Fox** is*
*trapped by Hell's mouth. The **Nun's Priest** blows a*
whistle to stop them and grab attention.

Now Chantecleer showed a little bit of cunning.
The fox was tired out from this bout of running.

CHANTECLEER   Now Mister Fox

NUN'S PRIEST   Said the wily bird.

CHANTECLEER   You must be groggy from all this din you've heard.
Now listen sir, if I were in your place,
I'd turn around and stand to, face to face.
Tell them that you've reached your safe, warm den,
Instruct them all to run away again.

NUN'S PRIEST   The fox missed Chantecleer's clever little joke,
And just as he opened wide and spoke,
The cock flew clear, safe and sound at last.
*(**Chantecleer** escapes and runs to the bedroom*
station.)
The fox could only utter:

FOX   Damn and blast.

Come down, sweet Chantecleer. I only carried you off so you could be my friend and sing to me, I swear.

CHANTECLEER   Balderdash! You were going to eat me. *(**Fox** leaves.)*

NUN'S PRIEST   And Chantecleer strutted back to his friends and family.

SCHOLAR   The moral?

NUN'S PRIEST   There are many.

HOST   Don't listen to women.

NUN'S PRIEST   Don't be deceived by flattery.

CHANTECLEER   Don't close your eyes to sing.

CHAUCER   Don't open your mouth before thinking carefully.

CHANTECLEER   Pay attention to dreams.

NUN'S PRIEST   Don't give in to your fate. Use all your cunning to survive.

All the cast sit around the stage.

HOST   *(Takes centre stage.)* We've had the lot tonight: the good, the bad,
The downright funny and the rather sad.
At least we haven't had tales that were boring,
I've not seen signs of anybody snoring.
But if we're going to buy someone a dinner
I'll have to ponder and declare a winner. *(Ponders.)*
The Pardoner's tale was moral all right –
It's a pity the teller is such a shite.
The Friar sent the Summoner to hell,
But he'll surely be going there as well.
The Miller's was a beaut, but rude, by gum!
I like the bit about the blistered bum.
The Reeve showed students in a better light
And had a thieving miller battered in a fight.
I praise the good Wife for her strong, firm views
And making sure that women get their dues.

And Chantecleer was a hero among cocks
For tricking the sly and crafty fox.
It's hard to choose – I'm getting in a tizz.
So you say Chaucer, who your winner is.

Chaucer and Scholar come forward.

CHAUCER That's something I'd dearly love to do,
But I much regret I haven't a clue.
As fate would have it, and the damndest luck,
I passed away before I could end the book.
But you've all heard them. Let's not act the goat:
We all can choose – let's put it to the vote.

SCHOLAR Hold on – I've got a better way to do it.
I like the book: I've read the whole way through it.
(And look what's happened – I knew it would in
time –
I've started speaking in a kind of rhyme.)
Since one man's written everything we've heard
Inventing Miller, Reeve, the fiends, the fox, the bird,
And even those of you who told each fable,
He's the one should be our guest at table.
As far as I'm concerned, and to my eyes,
It's Geoffrey Chaucer should collect the prize.

HOST By Saint Thomas, what a good idea.
I'll accept that, it's all so clear!
He's the man who should eat and sup.
If you lot pay, I'll serve it up.

The rest of the cast lead Chaucer out.

And all you listeners, God's blessing go to you,
While I takes the money from this motley crew.
God speed you in your travels, near and far –
But if you're staying, I'll see you in the bar.

He leaves. Blackout.

THE END

ACTIVITIES

THINGS TO TALK ABOUT

1 Keith Hurst's play starts with a scholar in modern dress reading *The Canterbury Tales*. He is quickly joined by Geoffrey Chaucer himself – a writer who died 600 years ago!

   • Talk about how, by inventing the character of the Scholar, the playwright helps the audience understand the background to the stories.

   • Skim through the play again, picking out the other times when the Scholar speaks. How else does he help the audience understand the tales?

2 In the original production of this version of *Canterbury Tales*, a male actor played the Wife of Bath and a female actor played Chantecleer. Read the introduction to the Wife of Bath's Tale again (pages 43–44) and also the way Chanticleer is introduced on pages 52–53. What sort of effect could casting the characters like this have on the way the audience would respond to them?

   Several of the stories are about relationships between men and women, and seem to make comments about attitudes towards sex and the different sexes. Talk about how having males playing other female parts and vice versa could:

   • add humour to a production;

   • draw the audience's attention to these attitudes.

3 Which moments of the play do you think an audience might enjoy most? You need to imagine what they would see and hear on the stage, and think about how those moments could be acted out. Talk about how you would want to stage those moments to make them really effective.

4 Some of the Canterbury Tales are often considered to be quite rude. Other people might think of them

as being 'great literature' and too difficult for school students to understand and enjoy. Perhaps some will find it surprising that this play was first performed in a community college.

- Do you think this play is suitable for young people?

- How would you justify putting on a play with so many 'rude' bits?

- Would you want to take a part in a performance or go and watch it – or would you find it embarrassing?

5   Chaucer's language looks quite different from modern-day English. It is called 'Middle English', and may at first sight seem hard to understand.

- Read the opening of the Introduction. Talk about the words that seem strange, and what they might mean.

- Read the section again out loud. Try putting on a number of different regional accents this time – Irish, Scottish, North Country, 'Mummerset' (a sort of general 'yokel' accent!).

Now, without worrying about the exact meaning of every word, talk about the general gist of what is being said in this introduction.

6   In small groups, read the last part of the Miller's Tale, pages 34–36. Again, try using different accents for the speeches written in Middle English. Talk about:

- why you think the playwright decided to switch from Modern to Middle English at these particular moments;

- whether this might make the play harder for the audience to understand, or if it might add to their enjoyment in some way.

7   Chaucer wrote a prologue to *The Canterbury Tales* in which he gave a brief description of each of the pilgrims. The tales that follow seem to suit the characters that tell them. The Miller, for example, is described as 'A great stout fellow, big in brawn and bone'. He had a bushy red beard, a hairy wart on his nose and big black nostrils. He also had a habit of knocking doors off their hinges by using his head as a battering ram, and telling filthy jokes. The Reeve doesn't like the Miller, and his description of the crooked Simkin seems designed to insult him personally.

What impressions do you have of the other characters? Write a brief description of one of them that would help an actor play the part. Say what you think they should look and sound like, how they act, and the effect they have on others.

8   The works of Chaucer may not immediately appeal to a modern audience to whom they are unfamiliar.

- Make some notes on aspects of this play that you think would appeal to audiences today.

- Imagine you have been asked to write a 'press release' advertising a production of the play for the local radio station. They can only give you 30 seconds of airtime, so what you say must be punchy and to the point. Use your notes to write the press release, then time yourself reading it aloud.

9   Much of *Canterbury Tales* is written in rhyming couplets and has a basic bouncy rhythm to it.

- Write an invitation to a production of the play using this sort of rhythm and rhyme.

- Write a short piece of dialogue in which two or

three of the characters from the play are talking in the bar after the performance, about the show and the stories they've heard. Again, the dialogue should follow the same rhythm and rhyme scheme as Chaucer's original.

BRINGING THE PLAY TO LIFE

10 There are several moments in the play when a character speaks directly to the audience, for example when the Host first enters on page 11. This technique, which is called 'direct address', is used to make the audience feel part of the show. For the technique to work, though, the actor needs to give every member of the audience the impression that they are being spoken to personally. This takes quite a lot of practice!

- In a group of around ten people, sit in a semi-circle. One person starts to tell a story. It might be a joke, or simply a description of their journey to school. They must try to make eye-contact with everyone while they are telling the story.

- If any member of the 'audience' feels that they have been left out for too long, they stand up. The storyteller must then make eye contact with them immediately while continuing with the story.

- A useful extension task would be to learn one of the speeches, for example the Wife of Bath's speech about her husbands (page 44), and try to deliver this to a group in way that makes them feel they are all being spoken to personally.

11 As well as the main characters who appear in the play, a group of Fiends make frequent appearances. Sometimes their job is to drag people off to Hell's mouth. At other times they become a part of the scenery.

- Read the description of Hell's mouth on page 12. Work in small groups to devise a sequence of movements and sound that would create a nightmarish atmosphere as people are dragged off to Hell.

- In the Friar's tale, the Fiends become the wood. Work as a whole group to make a spooky wood. Think about what sounds and movements could be used to suggest such a place.

- What other scenes could be brought to life on stage by having the Fiends use sound and movement to generate an appropriate atmosphere? For example, what contribution could they make to Chanticleer's nightmare on page 53?

12 Various animals such as horses and chickens are mentioned in the script. How could these parts be played by actors in an amusing and practical way? In pairs or small groups, devise a short sequence of movements which suggest a particular type of animal. Concentrate on facial expressions and ways of walking, rather than on imitating sounds. Consider how simple props might be used. In the original production, Chanticleer's comb was an inflated rubber glove and his hens/wives sported yellow pom-poms as wings with frogmen's flippers on their feet.

STAGING THE PLAY

At the time Chaucer was writing, one way of presenting plays would have been to have had wagons showing different scenes moving around the town rather like 'floats' in a modern-day carnival. Even in a static production, the audience's attention was drawn to different 'stations' which were set up around the performance space, rather than having one stage and lots of changes of scenery.

Hell, in particular, was an ever-present feature in the medieval mind. It was often presented as the mouth of a giant monster. The dead and the damned were taken through it by actors representing devils wearing firecrackers sticking from various parts of their bodies. Talking about the original production, Keith Hurst writes:

Since Hell was such a huge idea in the medieval mind, and since the Canterbury pilgrims would have believed in it and feared it (it's one reason why they went on a pilgrimage in the first place), I decided to have a Hell's mouth as the centre-piece of the action. This was a papier-mâché face, horned and fanged, big enough for fiends to take corpses through, mounted on a block of scaffolding. This was at one side of an apron or thrust stage, and at appropriate moments it would glow red and become the focus for fireworks and explosions. At the other end of the stage was a block of scaffolding which served as the bedroom in the Miller's tale and as a podium for the storytellers. It became referred to as the bedroom station or scaffold.

13 Draw a sketch or plan to show how you would position these 'stations' in your performance space. You will also need a flexible empty space where various scenes can be quickly set up and acted out.

14 Skim through the play paying particular attention to stage directions which suggest different locations. Draw up a simple chart, like the one on the next page, to show these places and how they might be represented simply in the empty performance space.

Location	Staging ideas
An inn	Fill stage with actors carrying pewter mugs. Some sit on three-legged stools. Wenches carry around trays or jugs of beer, etc.
Woods	Fiends carrying branches adopt poses of fairy-tale wood.
Apothecary's shop	Two actors (fiends?) crouch down as trestles. Apothecary puts a 'table top' onto them. Coloured bottles and chemistry equipment is fixed to the top.

15 In a number of scenes the actors need to time their actions very carefully with the storyteller's narration of the scene. For example, the Reeve's description of the drunken goings-on in Miller Simkin's bedroom (pages 40–43) or the poisoning scene in the Pardoner's tale. In groups, rehearse one of these scenes, or one of your own choosing, and concentrate on fitting the story to the 'stage-business'.

16 Make up a props list for a production of *Canterbury Tales*. The stage directions will give you some idea of what is needed, but you will also need to think about the characters and situations in order to draw up a comprehensive list. Plot your list on a table like the one on the opposite page, to make it clear when the prop is needed and by whom:

Scene	Prop	Character responsible
Introduction	Book Tea towel, beer mug Long toasting forks	Scholar Host Fiends
Pardoner's Tale	Cloth money bag, cheap cross Tankards, jugs, cards Scythe Hand cart	Pardoner Rioters Death figure Fiends
Friar's Tale	?	?

17 What sort of costumes would you need for a production of this play? Would you want to provide detailed period costumes for all of the characters? Or could they be represented in a simpler and perhaps cheaper way? In the original production, for example, the fox was clothed in black and armed only with a feather-duster tail.

Choose one character who you think should have a particularly interesting costume. Draw or describe their costume and say why you think it is important that this character stands out on the stage.

THE TALE OF CANTERBURY

Canterbury is the home of Christianity in Britain. Its Archbishop is the head of the Church of England. At the time Chaucer was writing, the Archbishop of Canterbury held an enormously powerful political position. He was thought of as the King's most direct route to God – if the King upset the Archbishop there could be all sorts of trouble! Two hundred years before Chaucer started writing *The Canterbury Tales*, King Henry II had, or so he thought, a brilliant idea to stop the possibility of such trouble. He appointed his best friend Thomas Becket to the post. Unfortunately for Henry, once Becket got the job he took his responsibilities very seriously, and refused to do everything that Henry wanted. Henry became so cross that he is alleged to have asked for someone to rid him of 'this troublesome priest'. Four of his knights did just that. They went to Canterbury and murdered Becket in the Cathedral. Becket was made a saint, and pilgrims began to visit his tomb in the hope and belief that doing so would bring them a blessing.

The story of Thomas Becket is the subject of two other well known plays. *Murder in the Cathedral* was written by the poet T. S. Eliot in 1935. *Becket*, by the French writer Jean Anouilh, was first staged in 1961, and made into a film starring Richard Burton and Peter O'Toole in 1964.

18   Look up Becket and Canterbury on the Internet. Try to find out more about:

- why Becket became a saint;

- the pilgrims who went to Canterbury;

- how his story has been told in films, plays, books and paintings.

19   At the time Chaucer was writing *The Canterbury Tales* England only had a population of around 2¹/₂ million people (today, London alone has around 8 million) – but travel was relatively easy because the stone-paved highways the Romans had built connected the major cities such as Canterbury, York, Chester and London. Although there were no permanent theatre buildings in England, a great many people would have seen some sort of play. Pageants, which involved re-telling the stories of the Bible on wagons which were moved around the town, were popular. Some of these 'mystery plays' still survive.

Do some research into the theatre of the Middle Ages, and make notes on how your research could be used to help a production of this play look and feel authentic. In particular, look up:

- the mystery plays;
- pageants and pageant wagons;
- the medieval theatre in the round;
- staging plays in church.

CHAUCER'S LIFE AND WORK

Geoffrey Chaucer was born in London in 1340. His father was a successful wine maker and could afford to give him a good education. He became a page to the Countess of Ulster, and this soon led to his being introduced to some of the most powerful people in the country. While serving as a soldier in 1359 he was captured by the French, who ransomed him – which shows how valued he already was in the court. On his return to England he took up a number of political and administrative posts, but always wrote.

He probably started writing *The Canterbury Tales* around 1387. He wrote them in order to read them aloud to the court, and it is still true that reading the stories aloud brings them to life in a way that reading them silently does not.

In the Prologue, Chaucer describes a meeting of 29 pilgrims in the Tabard Inn, Southwark, where Harry Bailly, the landlord, has the idea of a storytelling competition to pass the time on the way to Canterbury and back. Chaucer's idea seems to have been to have each pilgrim telling four tales each – two on the way there and two on the way back. However, only 23 pilgrims get to tell a story, with Chaucer adding two of his own.

The pilgrims Chaucer invented represent a wide range of medieval society. There are a number of tradesmen, such as the Haberdasher, the Weaver and the Carpet-maker; various religious people like the Nun, the Monk, the Friar and the Parson; and others from across the social spectrum: the Knight and his Squire, a Merchant, a Cook, a Skipper, a Ploughman and a Doctor.

Some of those on the journey would be unfamiliar to us today. For example:

A **friar** was a member of a Holy Order. He was licensed to beg in return for giving people blessings.

A **pardoner** could also bring forgiveness to sinners for a price. Pardoners sold pardons from the Pope. People bought 'indulgences' from them. For example, buying the finger bone of a saint would allow you to commit a certain number of sins before God took any notice. The higher the price you paid for such a holy relic, the more sins you would be allowed to commit.

A **reeve** would manage the estate of a wealthy person. This would probably mean being quite hard on poor tenants in order to maximise the profits for the estate owner.

A **summoner** had the job of bringing sinners to the church court. The job was open to abuse because it was often up to the summoner to decide who he thought was a sinner – which meant he could take bribes to forget about it!

A **yeoman** would serve a knight and his squire, but would be a trusted and respected soldier.

20 Research further into life in Chaucer's time, and his work. Use your findings to write a set of programme notes that would help a modern-day audience understand:

- who the different characters in the play were

- why Chaucer's work was so popular at the time

- how England and society was different 600 years ago from today.

21 Society in Chaucer's day was certainly very different from today. The Church had far more power and importance than it now seems to have. However, this did not necessarily mean that people in Chaucer's time were better behaved or kinder to each other then than they are now – *The Canterbury Tales* seems to illustrate that very clearly! To what extent do you think these stories still have an interest and important message for a modern audience? Either discuss this as a class or write your own programme note explaining why you think *The Canterbury Tales* have been popular for so long.